A Love

Letter

Pocket Guide to

Values

By Charles Wilson

Dedicated to my heirs

Prologue

"Man, Mr. Wilson, I swear I ain't been smokin'. I just smell like this 'cuz my cousin be smoking in the car. He the only one that can drop me off at school. My momma can't drive and my daddy ain't there. I can't make him stop smokin', but he my only way to school."

This is what Larry told me when I met him and the security staff at the school's entrance. He was being detained and denied access because of the smell of marijuana emanating from his clothing.

This high school had contracted me to run my intervention program, the Legacy Nexus Program. I had been working there for nearly three weeks with students the school deemed "ultra-high-risk youth." They kept this group of about twenty-five young boys and girls, who ranged from freshmen to seniors, in a room for the entire school day. Lunch for the students and the teachers themselves were brought to the classroom daily. Security guards escorted the students to the restroom. There was a security guard posted outside of their classroom at all times. They couldn't leave the room until the end of the school day.

I was called on the school's intercom because Larry asked for me. When I arrived, the security detail shared that Larry said he was one of my mentees and that I knew he didn't smoke weed. I shared that he was, in fact, a "Legacy student" and that I would bear responsibility for him for the rest of the day. Larry needed me to vouch for him. After they permitted him entry, we walked together to his first class, and he thanked me as he entered the classroom. I saw him later in the afternoon as we conducted our group intervention session. He thanked me again as he and his classmates were dismissed for the day.

At 7:58 that evening, I received a call from the school's Program Coordinator. With her voice thick with emotion and cracking, she informed me that Larry was killed about thirty minutes before our call. He entered a known dope house and robbed the occupants of product and money at gunpoint. When he left the home and was running away, the occupants he robbed grabbed a sawed-off shotgun and chased him down, shooting him in the back multiple times, killing him. He was sixteen years old.

News of his death made it to the *Chicago Sun-Times* the next day. The write-up was three sentences in total. His body stayed above ground for three weeks at the Cook County Examiner's office because his family couldn't afford to bury him. I called a personal associate at a local funeral home who agreed to lay him to rest for the family.

Can you teach values?

Absolutely, that's why we are the way we are. Our values reflect a learned set of behaviors. What we feel guilty about, feel apologetic for, feel aloof about, feel offended by — are all based in the value system taught to us by those we've encountered along our personal growth journey.

The greatest impact on our development occurs when we are children, and is molded, contrasted, and tugged by meaningful experiences as we continue to mature into the person we face in the mirror each day.

A parent, guardian, mentor or other person who (willingly or unwillingly) takes up the responsibility of shaping the values of another, has to be intrusive and deliberate, because a child or a person left to "figure it out" on their own will not have learned the values and behaviors that will help them succeed in life.

Someone has to care enough to have tough conversations with them to help guide them.

Parents and guardians have to be patient and accept that children may get upset with them when these tough conversations occur. The parents and guardians may get frustrated in return, but they can't abandon the responsibility of establishing guideposts in their children's lives. They must love enough to help lay a foundation that will open doors and provide them with opportunities to create a more desirable life, filled with everything they've dreamed of or imagined for themselves.

I wrote *A Love Letter* to my own children, who range in age from youth to young adults, to reinforce the values I have.

I was eighteen when I had my first child, and I remember facing each decision I had to make based on what I would want someone to do for me. I only understood what I wanted and what I valued based on what my mother, and those whom she allowed to invest in my development, instilled in me. And what they instilled in me was based on what was instilled in them, and so on, and so on.

The thing is, I don't want to wait until I'm about to die, or I have somehow reached this "Yoda-like," stratospheric level of wisdom and maturity, before I give my children my personal journal, of sorts. I want them to reference something they know describes the make-up and the core principles of their father. I want them to call me out on any hypocrisy I may exhibit in my life. I want them to reap the benefits of doing things the certain way, now. I want their children, and *their* children's children, to know the man who taught their parents and poured the best version of himself into them.

I want my children's friends to get a glimpse into how I created the cast that has molded the people they've grown to know. I want my friends, teachers, mentors, and family to know how they've influenced me and see how I've woven their pearls of wisdom in the fabric used to raise my heirs.

Finally, I want those responsible for the lives of others and those who are the "others," who feel they don't have an anchor in their lives to help them feel settled enough to form a stable foundation, to have a guide I pray adds value to them and helps shape their values.

Ultimately, for all who read this, I write this from the Love I have for you.

Guideposts to Values

There is no one better at being you.

You're the best.

We often feel pressure to conform to what other people deem "normal" behavior. These people who apply this pressure haven't lived with our experiences or in our exact environment.

What is "normal?" Who determines what is normal and what isn't? Why should you trust them to make that determination about you, your special skills and your capabilities? You are one of a kind, which means you have the power to create a brand new, "not normal," ANYTHING you focus your talents, efforts, and imagination into creating.

There are federal, state, and local laws that govern some of your outward expressions and actions. These laws don't inhibit your creativity, though. In fact, they challenge you to become even more creative in sharing your uniquely crafted gift with the world. Your creative imagination is the vehicle by which you will deliver your talent.

You are the best at what you do.

How can anyone be a better you when there is no other person like you? So, by default, you are the best. Live like it. Whatever you invest your time and talent in, be *your* best.

Foundational Questions

- Are you proud of the person you see when you look in the mirror?

- Are you proud of the effort you put into your work, assignments, or purpose?

- Have you allowed someone else to define you?

Don't fear; it's just new

Fear has endurance. Scared is temporary. Fear prevents. Scared invigorates. Fear cuts off creativity. Scared focuses the senses and attention. Fear says: "It's over." Scared says: "It's just beginning."

We are human. Being startled or surprised when something unexpected occurs lets us know that we are alive and still able to sense and feel. Our sensory acknowledges that there are variables that occur around us that may not be in our control. These variables make the conditions we find ourselves in new to us.

When something expected happens, we don't experience the same internal feelings. We aren't awakened. We move through the experience with a sense of comfort and ease because of the sense of familiarity. When something has happened before, like watching a movie for a second or third time, the surprise ending is no longer, well, a surprise.

My charge is for you to take the Initial Step into something new. It's okay to be scared because you don't know what to expect. It's okay to look around and for everything to feel unfamiliar. It's okay to be the first or the only one. The focus,

determination, and creativity you will feel
will be its own natural reward.

When you take that Initial Step,
your assumptions get debunked or
validated. You mature. You gain
experiences. The "new" becomes familiar,
and you gain the opportunity to hone your
talent and skills. You build your aptitude.

Fear impedes your expansion. It's a
thief. Once a thief thinks he or she can get
away with the theft, more often than not,
the thief will come back for more. Fear will
spread and rob you of other aspects of your

life where expansion and growth should occur.

"What if," will always be present. You already know what the current situation feels like. You're in it. Just take the Initial Step. Be prepared for exhilaration and the personal sense of accomplishment that comes with no need for outside validation. You will know that you've defeated fear and will want to replicate that feeling again and again.

Foundational Questions

- How long will you allow that invisible enemy, fear, to prevent you from taking the Initial Step?

- When will you decide that you are the only person holding you back?

- What or who are you waiting for to give you the courage you already have laying dormant inside you?

Keep loving

Love was never intended to stay bottled up. Its genesis is within you. Recognizing the love you have for yourself creates the template for how you will express love to others. To love means to have a sense of the value of who or that which is to be loved. Who or that which is to be loved has to have meaning. Since the genesis of love starts within you, *you* need to have a sense of value and meaning to *yourself.*

In your physical growth and development as a person, there came a time when you realized your decisions impacted

22

others. That impact made you feel something which was desirable or undesirable. You enjoyed the outcomes, or you didn't. You wanted that feeling again, or you didn't want that feeling again.

Those feelings helped establish your values. The importance of the decisions you made started to take form based on the feelings you had when interacting with others.

Why do I share that love is not intended to stay bottled up? Because the feelings you received from those outcomes as you were being introduced to the decision-outcome relationship as a child, were shaped by those who raised you. They provided you with the boundaries you needed to grow and develop as a person.

Whatever those individuals valued in their lives became the template for the development of your value system. Your decisions fostered a reward or a punishment, and those individuals established the choice. Reciting your ABC's, or tying your shoe, or pooping on the potty all fostered some reward. Claps and smiles, cookies or juice, kisses on the cheek or tickling were positive outcomes that encouraged you to repeat the behavior.

These rewards motivated you to seek other areas and challenges that could yield similar or greater rewards when you made accomplishments.

Some people only received punishment when they didn't accomplish a goal or task set by those who raised them. The reward for them was to simply avoid punishment.

Therefore, some people can go throughout their lives, not knowing how to love. They don't know how to love because of how their values were shaped. They may not know how to love themselves because they weren't groomed to see themselves as valuable or having meaning.

Hurt and pain may be all they know. It's possible for you to be the first person to show them what love is. Your expression of love for yourself — by your self-care, confidence, and fearlessness — may become the new template they use to expand their own value system. Rewarding them for their accomplishments and for making good decisions may be the incentive they need to repeat the behavior or actions.

When you keep loving, you can create a chain reaction that can positively shape individual lives, families, communities, states, and countries. Don't bottle it up. Give the love you have and let it go. Watch the wonders it creates.

Foundational Questions

- Who in your life have you kept love from?

- Who has impacted your ability to trust others?

- How long will you surrender your power and allow them to be the excuse as to why you won't give your love?

- Who do you blame for hurting or disappointing you, causing you to close yourself off to others?

Stop blaming

Blame is low hanging fruit; easy to get to. It absolves you of the accountability you should own. It shapes your skill in the art of deflection. When those who are always seeking to create solutions, hear someone blaming someone or something else for whatever may be an undesirable outcome, it burns their ears. Blame disqualifies those who use it and prevents them from being considered "wise" or good investments.

The outcomes you feel and experience are a direct result of the decision or series of decisions you made.

How could you shape your mind to create an argument based on sound premise and still have concluded that it's "someone else's fault" when that decision presents an undesirable outcome?

When you blame others for your failed decisions, you relinquish the power your mind has to be creative and your ability to harness that power to live in the reality you so desire.

Your blame should be replaced with gratitude. Gratitude comes with understanding and accepting the truth of that power you possess. I give you this prayer gratitude to recite and to use as a reset each day: *Thank you for the gift of thought and the power to control that thought for the attainment of whatever it is I desire to obtain.*

Blame is your willing relinquishment of power. You are never powerless. You've just restrained your thoughtful creativity. Accept the outcomes of the decisions you make and create a new reality so that you build from them, not blame.

- Have you limited the ability of your mind so much that you see no other way to find success?

- With my definition of *success* being, "the attainment of a specific goal or set of goals," will you allow a person who may have delivered a temporary setback or unexpected hurt and pain, defeat you?

- If you can read these questions and can ask them of yourself, can't you see that you are not defeated?

Keep giving

Giving creates multiplication. Just know that the more you give, the more you'll receive. It'll be in ways you never imagined, and you didn't plan for. But give, because you have it to give, not based on what you want to receive. That part takes care of itself.

When you give of your gifts and talents, there is a succinct set of actions that go into motion. This is beyond religion or dogmas. I know this based on my own experiences and what I have witnessed of others who do things a certain way.

Like the Merry-Go-Round that spins when you insert a coin, the universe puts things in motion for your ultimate benefit when you pay its toll. Everything moves and you get to enjoy those benefits.

When you give of your gifts, you will receive all of the provisions you need to cultivate, nurture, and continue to give. The universe creates the environment of these provisions for you. It's as automatic as spring is for seeds planted in the fall. The seed knows that it will blossom and flourish into the plant, tree, fruit, or vegetable it inevitably becomes. It does its part by being where it's supposed to be for nature to do its part.

For example, if the seed "decided" to come up to see what was happening during the winter and didn't wait for the rain and warm sun of the spring, it would kill its own potential and growth.

Move in anticipation of. Expect that when you're doing your part, the universe will do its part to multiply you. Don't be afraid of the cold and darkness that comes.

Push through those dark periods when they come in your life. Those periods take the shape of doubt, disbelief, fear, lack of confidence, and discouragement. Keep doing your part, and the conditions and opportunities for your gifts to flourish will present themselves. Just as the new plant, tree, fruit, and vegetable creates more seeds in its new form, you can expect more gifts to form inside of you in order for you to continue to give. Giving multiplies.

Foundational Questions

- What do you wish someone had told you or showed you that you now want everyone else to know so they don't have to go through the same?

- What experience(s) have you had that others have used to define you as someone negative; yet has the power to give hope and encouragement to others?

- Have you lost your faith in your pursuit to attain a goal you haven't yet attained?

- Have you given up too soon?

- Aren't you worth giving yourself another chance to add value to others?

Add value

Challenge yourself to be a person who helps others become the best version of themselves. With any appreciable amount of time a person spends with you and talks with you, there should be an accompanying sense of responsibility you feel in helping them become the best version of themselves. As you seek this challenge, you are being the best version of yourself.

This challenge helps you establish a mindset of adding value. People should be able to observe your decision-making process and desire to implement it in their own process. People should walk away from an encounter with you and have a time of introspection of their own lives. When you add value, you inspire others to love a little more, care a little more, give a little more, be more accountable, stop blaming a little more, and be more courageous.

We often hear of people being grouped as "Givers" or "Takers." There is another segment of people who are positive reciprocals of Givers: Receivers. Receivers differ from Takers in that Receivers are the free-willed, intended target of the Giver.

Whatever is provided to Receivers is meant for them.

"Giving" to a Receiver is an expression of gratitude or reward. However, Receivers are usually hesitant or resistant to accept the expression or reward. Givers are so focused on releasing their gifts, they rarely look back or desire to be Receivers. When they look back, they are typically inspecting their impact to determine what else they may need to give. They don't desire to ask for help or to delegate. They feel an immense sense of responsibility for completing a task or fulfilling of a commitment they've made.

41

I desire for you to be Givers. You find that by default, you will become Receivers. It won't be difficult. You won't have to seek it out. Your gifts and rewards will find you. Your impact will be felt and will create positive, long-term effects and ripples that you could never have imagined.

At times, those impacted by your giving will not know how to express their gratitude. They will sometimes feel that their gifts or rewards can't measure up to what you gave them.

So, when they give to you, honor them by accepting it. Even in your acceptance, you are still giving. The feelings of personal fulfillment you'll experience with this mindset will be euphoric. You will feel emptied and yet satisfied. This is because you'll know you added value.

Foundational Questions

- Have you been a Receiver or a Taker?

- Have people shared that they feel better or more positive because of you being in their lives?

- What's stopping you from becoming a value-add to others you interact with or influence?

- Do you know that you can be someone others can depend on when their own pathways to positivity seem dark or unclear to them?

It all matters. It's all perfect.

You're not a mistake. You were made by design. Everything was meant to be the way it is. So be flexible. Be nimble. Be creative. Use all the tools you already have within you. Make your life your own paradise, just the way you want it.

We can sometimes become discouraged by the process we have to endure to accomplish a goal. We may not like the "packaging" the attainment came in. We may despise the pathway the journey is calling for us to take. We sometimes feel that we didn't need the

45

scarring, bruising or hurt that came with the accomplishment.

I've felt, many times, that I would have been just as enlightened by learning from other people's mistakes. I've felt like: "Why do I need to go through the same crap?! I can see that the fire will burn me if I touch it!"

The only way you can come to appreciate, accept and understand that it all matters and it's all perfect, is if you accept that you're a Giver and there is no one to blame. There are outcomes from the decisions we make. That's all they are.

Adapt and bend as necessary. Your decisions got you here. So, own the outcomes.

There is a point before we do something, where we come to a fork in the road. We encounter this point multiple times a day and in years. We are living in a continuous decision-making tree.

Ask yourself at these forks in the road: "Is what I am about to gain, worth what I might lose?" No other person can know what you value more, better than you. Others may have their opinions or assumptions, but they cannot know what impact your experiences have on your value system. When you have resolved what your decision will be, and then act on it, you set in motion the EXACT outcome from that decision.

You have an internal desire for what the outcome will bear. The creation of the outcome is where your tools come into play. This creation requires you to adapt and bend. This is when the lens by which you look at the process, pathway or packaging has to be adjusted to clearly see what needs to be done to achieve your goal.

You'll find that impatience will yield undesirable outcomes. It's like the planted seed that tries to sprout in winter. When you've peeked your head out too soon during the process, it's another decision you've made which has set into motion what is meant to be.

So, it all matters. Every traffic light you "missed" while driving to a job interview. Every flight delayed on your way to vacation. Every relationship that began or ended. Every morning you didn't exercise. Every time you felt the confidence and acted. It all mattered. It set in motion a perfect process by which we realize outcomes. The only thing that changes is how you perceive those outcomes.

No one can control your thoughts. So, care about what you're thinking. You create everything that's your reality because reality is a manifestation of thoughts. What you physically see each day is the outward expression of someone's thoughts — all from God or from us as extensions of God. What outward expression will you create?

- Do you realize that your experiences are not the final judgment for how wonderful your life can be?

- Did you know that only you control the safety and security of your mind?

- Will you allow your thoughts to be the seeds for your new life filled with actual physical realities created by your imagination?

- Will you take the time to consider all the outcomes for the decisions you make? And once you have

considered those outcomes, will you
ask yourself: "Is this action worth
feeling the pain of the potential
negative outcomes I may
experience, all so I can feel the
potential positive outcomes I desire
to experience?"

- Do you believe you are valuable
  enough to care about the outcomes?

Now, is a good time

Conditions will never be more perfect than they are now. Now is the time you are inspired to think the thoughts you are thinking. Now is the time that your gears are turning. Your imagination is crafting the vehicle by which your thoughts will eventually translate to reality. Your excitement, curiosity, adrenaline, and neurons are all firing in what seems to be an internal fireworks display. And you love it!

Your inner voice is a powerful ally. It is the true you that is part of the bigger, unseen universe. It is what makes up your soul. It has no boundaries or physical rules it abides by. It sees and delivers messages of growth and abundance to you. It doesn't have any other way to be or to act. It is courageous. It is wise and intuitive. It is free.

And then, you go messing with it. Debating it. Restraining it. "Disciplining" it to make sure whatever instruction or direction being given doesn't buck the norm or make you seem "crazy."

We live in a world governed by laws and social norms. Certain activities have real consequences that can cost you money, take your freedom, or end your life. But that creative inner voice is wise. It takes this into account and shows you how to flourish within the realm you live in. It shares ways for you to move freely about in this sphere that keeps all of us alive.

You are extraordinary. When your imagination sparks, you are ready to do what needs to be done to make your dreams a reality.

You have already interpreted and decoded the message(s) from your imagination and you are naturally programmed to **Do** whatever it has given you as an assignment. There are only so many times that you can ignore or silence your imagination before you create a new norm: complacency and delay.

When you are complacent or delay action, you will cause a "backup" of the messages your inner voice is trying to relay to you from your imagination. The imagination is continuously sending messages. But, if you do not act on your imagination, your imagination will shut down. It will only restart when what has already been delivered to you has been acted on. You cannot receive the new messages if you haven't performed the old.

If you don't process and act on the messages you receive in a timely manner, you may miss the window of opportunity that would've provided you with the greatest benefit.

Do and do it now.

Foundational Questions

- What or who are you waiting for?

- What are the perfect conditions you believe should be in place for you to do what you need to do?

- What are you doing to create the conditions you believe are necessary for you to be a doer?

- Have you made the lack of conditions you believe you need to be in place an excuse to not do it now?

- Are you and/or your fear driving your decisions?

- How many times will you ignore that inner voice that is guiding you on the best path forward for your life?

It's just stuff

Forget the stuff; go for the experiences. We try to capture moments instead of experiencing them. Be present. Be there. Why miss the action happening right in front of you, because you're recording it — especially when you will not have the same feeling when you view the recording later?

The exhilaration will never match up to the day you were there: feeling the wind, smelling the fragrances and aromas, feeling the bass from the speakers, or being surprised by the guest performer the headliner brought out during the concert.

These things happen right at the time that they are happening. Not later.

If acquiring "stuff" or the journey to acquiring it stresses you, map out a new destination. If the validation from others drives you to purchase stuff to fill a void inside of you, then you need to go back to the beginning of this letter. You need to be comfortable enough with yourself to know that you are enough. Period. This stuff will perish in your life and lose its value to you.

The feelings you get from experiences will leave an indelible imprint on your mind and heart. Become the author of your Feelings Journal. Enjoy the

freedom of turning each page of your life,

in your mind, and relive the greatest story

ever experienced.

- Do you desire to acquire stuff because it's what *you* want to enjoy, or do you want to acquire stuff so that others envy you?

- Once you've experienced having whatever it is you've acquired, are you willing to let it go if it stresses you mentally, physically, emotionally, or financially?

- Are you willing to let it go if it hinders your ability to live a full value-adding life?

- In your pursuit to acquire stuff, are you observing or experiencing people you love and care about, becoming distant or disconnected from you?

- In your pursuit to acquire stuff, are you missing special occasions and quality time with others, believing that you'll make it up to them some other time?

Relationships matter

There will be or already has come a time in your life where the outcome of a situation wasn't determined by what you know, but who you know. Just as in the case of Larry, no matter what he felt was his truth, he needed that truth to be validated when he was trying to enter the school. Larry needed to be vouched for.

Who knows you? Why should I trust you? Can I even believe you? What makes you so different from all the other people who have disappointed me in my life? These may be some of the questions you have asked of those who are in your

life or want to be in your life. They are

questions others have asked themselves of

you.

A key component for the success of

a relationship is vouching.

Vouching is critical when planning

(or not planning) to interact with anyone

other than yourself. Vouching is another

person's account or summarization of you

in a favorable light. When you're being

vouched for, the other person is validating

whatever positive claim you've made about

yourself or that another person has made

about you. The person who is vouching must have their own credibility and trust established so that their vouch has value. For example, there is no point in having a known liar share that you're the most truthful person they know.

When vouching occurs, there is a responsibility that lies between the person vouching and the person being vouched for. The person doing the vouching has to maintain a track record of trust and credibility.

The recipient of the vouch has a responsibility to meet or exceed those expectations dictated by the person who put their credibility and trust on the line for them. This is critical because you, as the recipient, have the power to damage their credibility and trust; resulting in their inability to use their vouch to help others who may be deserving.

We cannot accomplish anything prosperous in this life in complete isolation. We are fashioned to assemble, collaborate, create and co-exist with others. From our instructors to our guardians to our friends — our relationships matter. Those we have relationships with influence our decisions

and offer perspectives and insights we may
not otherwise see.

A boxer doesn't go to her corner
after a round without a trainer or coach
present who can share what the boxer
couldn't see in her performance. But just
like the boxer, who you have in your corner
can influence actions that could be to your
detriment or overall victory.

Be good stewards of your
relationships. Return to the question and
make it applicable in the selection of the
relationships you are engaged in. Ask

yourself: "Is what I am about to gain, worth what I might lose?"

Remember your value. Can you be vouched for? Recognize the value being brought to the table by the other. Can the other be vouched for? Analyze how you both may add value to the relationship. This is YOUR responsibility. When you take the time to do this, there will be no room for blame for any outcomes. You will understand why your relationships matter.

Foundational Questions

- Why is this person in your life?

- Why does this person want you in their life?

- Are you having *Expectations Conversations* with those you hope will add value to your life or when they believe you will add value to theirs?

- Are you being honest and truthful with yourself and the other person about your ability to meet their expectations?

- Are you more worried about losing the relationship if you're honest and truthful than of destroying the trust (and ultimately the relationship), once your deception is exposed?

- Are you ensuring that you are a good steward or keeper of a person's vouch for your character or values?

- Have you done your due diligence so you can vouch for this person with confidence?

- What or who in your life are you willing to sacrifice or lose in order to keep this relationship?

- Are your emotions or your reasoning driving your decision to pursue, maintain, or sever the relationship?

Epilogue

Legacy Commitment Statement

I am a Leader and an Innovator.

Through Visualization and Critical

Thinking,

I will accomplish whatever goal I set in my

mind.

My Legacy Has Begun.

"**I am**" is a proclamation of your self-actualization. You know it with certainty and it is intrinsic.

"**A Leader**" is one who influences others.

Being a leader doesn't rest in being in front

of the class, captain of the team, or a

department head. Those are roles.

Leadership is an observable behavior.

A person can lead from the middle

of the pack or from the receptionist desk.

Someone else could observe that you come

to work 30 minutes early each day and

desire to mimic your behavior. Others

could smell the perfume you're wearing

and want to smell like you. There may be a

person who has tasted a roast you've

cooked and share that they have always

wanted to make their roast taste like that.

We can overlook the seemingly smallest things, in our own minds, and find that they have had a significant influence on the behaviors and actions of others. So, what kind of leader will you be? It's easy to see how we have created those deemed "good" or "bad" leaders. Allow your values of giving and loving to continue, and you'll be regarded as good.

"**An Innovator**" is one who is aware of a process or creation that exists and improves the process or creation. You get a running start. If you're smart, you'll see this as a great advantage and of value to you.

We often want to originate whatever we put our efforts into. Unfortunately, and to your great surprise, you may not be the only smart person with great ideas who has lived. Most of the ideas we experience are a reiteration or recycled from something else. What you can take solace in is that this revised, reimagined, reinvigorated approach you have created *is* yours. Because of your uniqueness, your

77

imagination will differ from that of anyone else. You may find similarities in some ideas, but no one will have the exact idea you have. Remember that. Use this for your fuel and motivation as you encounter opportunities to leave your mark.

"**Visualization**" is your mind's ability to create a picture of your desire that is so vivid and real, that you smell the aroma, taste the flavor, and hear the sounds of whatever it is you desire. *You* create a specific, detailed outline of the physical equivalent of your desire. This is critical in your preparation to receive whatever it is you have visualized.

Visualization is your imagination revving the engines and putting in gear the faith required to carry you through doubt, fear, haters, and limitations. Nothing you see or experience in the "now" happened without visualization.

You have to consider that what we physically see started as a thought. All of it. People 200 years ago, if reborn and allowed to see what the world has become today, would deem this impossible, or the person who thought to create it was insane, a witch, or a god. You are in command of the limitations you put on your imagination.

"**Critical thinking**" requires you to be present. It also requires you to consider how your actions today will impact your future. It requires you to mentally operate in that which you've visualized and live as if all of what you visualized is happening. For instance, if you visualized you earned a million dollars, what would you do? What steps would you take to earn the money? How would you spend this new money? Who would be there with you? What if you didn't get the money when you thought you would? What if the money came from a place you didn't expect? Critical thinking is a necessity for longevity.

When you are pre-emptive instead of reactive, your journey in life is smoother with fewer bumps in the road. Moving in anticipation of that which you have visualized allows you a sneak peek into the next chapters of this metaphoric book you're writing of your life. It gives you the ability to put in place contingencies or guard rails. It allows a much softer landing as opposed to those who move without expectation or anticipation. Thinking critically puts a down payment on the bigness of your faith.

"I will accomplish whatever goal I set in my mind" is an affirmation that combines visualization and critical thinking. It is a process that works with certainty and is as absolute as the rising and setting of the sun. The key is to be specific about your goal.

If I, Charles Wilson, were to type into my phone's navigation system, "Somewhere," no map or pathway for me to get there would appear. But if I type in "Chicago" as my destination, it would lay the path out. At which point, I have to decide what mode of travel I desire to take or if I will take the trip at all.

You will face many crossroads throughout your life as you continue to develop and specify your goals. You may sometimes find that there are "offramps" and "detours" that you didn't know existed. You may encounter people and opportunities that you otherwise would not have known existed had you not charted this path you're traveling to accomplish your goals.

The effort in accomplishing will create growth and multiplication to the plan. Just keep your Eyes Forward. Looking behind you for those things you cannot undo or bring back is a waste if you don't use them as opportunities to build or learn. The experiences of the past are opportunities, not restraints and baggage. But, the choice in viewing the experiences of the past as fuel and motivation, instead of excuses for why you will or will not accomplish a goal you've set, is up to you and the lens through which you view them.

"My Legacy has begun" is a realization that each time you wake up and interact with someone or something outside of yourself, you are furthering your Legacy. Your Legacy is how people will remember you. The thoughts that come to mind when people recall you in their memories. It's the foundation you've laid for those who come after you to build upon in the establishment of their own Legacies.

When you know you can add value and how you can add value, your Legacy has begun. Each day that you're aware is a day that your Legacy is molded, rooted, and grounded in the values you believe in

and establish.

What will your Legacy be?

For me, Charles Wilson: I am reasonable,

empathetic, loving and continuously

striving to be magnanimous.

54342166R00054

Made in the USA
Middletown, DE
13 July 2019